My Little Golden Book About
# ABRAHaM LiNCOLN

by Bonnie Bader

illustrated by Viviana Garofoli

The editors would like to thank Ian Patrick Hunt, Historian, Abraham Lincoln Presidential Library Foundation, for his assistance in the preparation of this book.

A GOLDEN BOOK • NEW YORK

Text copyright © 2016 by Bonnie Bader
Illustrations copyright © 2016 by Viviana Garofoli
All rights reserved. Published in the United States by Golden Books, an imprint of Random House Children's Books, a division of Penguin Random House LLC, 1745 Broadway, New York, NY 10019, and in Canada by Penguin Random House Canada Limited, Toronto. Golden Books, A Golden Book, A Little Golden Book, the G colophon, and the distinctive gold spine are registered trademarks of Penguin Random House LLC.
randomhousekids.com
Educators and librarians, for a variety of teaching tools, visit us at
RHTeachersLibrarians.com
Library of Congress Control Number: 2015947389
ISBN 978-1-101-93971-0 (trade) — ISBN 978-1-101-93972-7 (ebook)
Printed in the United States of America
10 9 8 7 6 5 4 3 2 1

# ABRAHAM LINCOLN WAS ONE OF OUR COUNTRY'S GREATEST PRESIDENTS.

From the time he was a little boy, Abe was a hard worker. He helped on his parents' farm, planting corn and pumpkins.

Abe and his sister, Sarah, went to school in a one-room schoolhouse. They walked for miles to get there and back, even in snow. Abe studied hard. He learned to read and write. Abe loved to learn, and he read every book he could find.

When Abe was seven, his family moved to the settlement of Little Pigeon Creek, Indiana. Abe learned to use an ax. He helped his father clear the forest for a farm and a cabin. There was no longer time for school. Since Abe always had to work to help his family survive, his total schooling added up to less than one year.

By the time Abe had finished growing,
he was very tall—six feet four inches!

Abe knew he didn't want to be a farmer like
his father. But what could he do? He decided
to leave home to find out.

Abe got a job on a flatboat. He was such a
good worker that the boat's owner offered him
a job in his store in New Salem, Illinois.

The people of New Salem quickly grew
to love and trust Abe. Abe was so honest that
once when he charged someone too much
money, he ran outside to give the money back.
Throughout his life, he had the nickname
Honest Abe.

People started to go into the
store just to ask Abe's advice.
Sometimes they asked him about
the laws or rules of the town.

Abe wanted to study more. So he studied
law—all by himself—and became a lawyer.

Abe moved to Springfield, Illinois, to work with a lawyer friend. One of Abe's jobs was to keep track of the lawyer's papers. He kept some of the papers inside his tall hat!

When Abe was twenty-eight, he met Mary Todd. Mary and Abe were different in many ways. Abe was tall and thin. Mary was short and plump. Abe came from a poor family. Mary came from a rich family. Although Abe was shy, the two fell in love. They married and had four children together.

At that time, white people were allowed in some states to own black slaves. The slaves were forced to work hard, and they did not get paid. They were not treated well. The slaves did not have any rights.

Abe spoke out against slavery. He became very famous. Some people asked Abe to run for president of the United States. Abe said yes.

Soon it was time for the people to vote. The votes were counted. And, surprise—Abe won!

The Lincoln family moved from Illinois to the White House in Washington, D.C. Abe greeted happy crowds on his whistle-stop train trip to Washington.

Everyone in the country loved the Lincoln boys! They were sent a lot of presents, including a pony and two goats. The goats got loose once inside the White House and made a mess during a fancy party!

But trouble was brewing. The people who lived in the states that allowed slavery did not like Abe. They said he was not their president. Eleven states broke away from the United States. They did not want to be part of a country that was against slavery. The United States was no longer united.

Now the country was at war—the Civil War.

More than anything, Abe
wanted to end slavery. "All men
are created equal," he declared.
Finally, he was able to help pass
a law to free the slaves.

Abe went to the battlefields and gave speeches to ask people to stop fighting. It took years for the Civil War to end.

Abe was constantly interrupted while he worked—and not just by his sons. Each day, people stood in long lines, waiting to speak with the president. They asked him for money, and for help finding jobs.

When the war was finally over, crowds of joyful people went to the White House to cheer for the president. Abe was proud that there was no more slavery. Now he had to bring the country back together.

Sadly, Abe died before the United States was fully united in peace.

# REMEMBERING ABRAHAM LINCOLN

Did you know that Abraham Lincoln was the tallest United States president—and the first president with a beard?

Lincoln made Thanksgiving a national holiday. And he signed a law that protected the beautiful land that later became Yosemite National Park.

Lincoln's face is on the penny and
the five-dollar bill. And it's carved into
Mount Rushmore, along with those of
three other popular presidents.

There is a memorial for Abraham Lincoln in Washington, D.C. It is called the Lincoln Memorial. Thousands of people visit it each year.

Abraham Lincoln will always be remembered as a smart man, a good listener, and a great president.